THE DEEPEST LAKE

*With a rope of loose-spun thread am I towing
My boat upon the river.
Would that God hear my prayers and bring me safe across!*

LALLESHWARI
14th century Sufi mystic Kashmiri poetess

Late October, 2014.

I am the only guest on a houseboat that is anchored in the middle of Dal Lake. I've just arrived in Srinagar, Kashmir to photograph a travel story for an American magazine. After a day and a half of travel, I'm disoriented. I carefully climb a steep flight of stairs to the roof deck of the houseboat; it is nearly sunset. The deck (like the rest of the houseboat) is empty aside from stacks of chaise lounges piled under a tarp. The travel season is ending in Srinagar; soon, it will be winter. However, the sunset feels warm and the light is pink and soft. I raise my camera to take a photo of the enormous lake in front of me and the Zabarwan mountains that frame it. A young shikara wallah paddles into the frame, and I press the shutter button. I will return to this view again and again over the following week.

While driving through the congested center of town the next day, we pass by two men digging a large pit alongside the road. It's deep; they are only visible from the chest up. Seven or eight other men stand around the ditch and observe. They don't look like supervisors; I think they are just curious bystanders. One of the bystanders says something and a few others laugh, but they all keep their eyes fixed on the men digging. On a different day, I watch a man nailing a long piece of wood over a hole in a fence. At least four others stand around him and watch.

I start to notice how much of life is lived communally here, in public and on the street. People stand outside their homes or on their balconies and watch the throng of motorbikes, cars and pedestrians. A group of men sit in front of a spice vendor and have a loud debate. There are people visible everywhere. Whereas at home in New York, the city feels composed of millions of individuals shut inside their offices and studio apartments, stacked on top of one another. Alone together.

In Srinagar, I take a photo of three schoolchildren standing on a bridge over the Jhelum River. The late afternoon sun glows in the distance. Seconds after I snap the photo, one of the girls slaps the boy across the face.

Early one foggy morning, we drive for two hours east towards the Aru Valley and the Himalayas. It's a major road but it is unpaved; there are at least four or five unmarked lanes. I can feel every bump and rut in the road. At times, the traffic is intense and drivers honk their horns constantly. Gulzar, my local guide, has a theory that Kashmiri men aggressively honk their horns in order to vent their latent frustration with a lack of political power in a conflict zone controlled by India and Pakistan. The car fills with dust and exhaust; I cover my mouth with my shirt and try to relax. Through the fog and clouds of dirt, I see distant paramilitary soldiers standing along the road. The soldiers have machine guns slung across their chests; they are spaced intermittently like telephone poles, keeping watch.

A few hours later, it is brilliantly sunny and quiet as we hike into the mountains. The alpine air is fresh; the sweeping landscape leaves me nearly speechless. I did not anticipate I would ever see the Himalayas. And here they are.

I learn that Kashmir has been considered a mystical paradise on earth for centuries. Anil, the Indian-American owner of my film lab in New York City, first told me this after I mentioned my imminent trip. Mughal emperors built palaces and spent their summers in the area that is now Srinagar; generations of people from India and all over the world have followed. We visit the Mughal gardens in Srinagar: *Nishat* (The Garden of Pleasure), *Shalimar* (The Garden of Love), *Nasim Bagh* (Garden of the Morning Breeze), and *Cheshma Shahi* (The Royal Spring). I'm sure these gardens are stunning when they are in full bloom in June and July, a riot of bright colors. But I like them in late October: the fallen chinar leaves scattered in the now-empty fountains, the muted and subtle colors of dying flowers in the raw morning fog. I stop and photograph the flowers in these gardens and in various courtyards all week; these flowers are a constant in the pictures I make here.

November, 2015.

I am choosing the final photographs to include in this book. I make inexpensive 4x6-inch prints so that I can lay everything out in front of me, moving and sequencing the photos like a deck of playing cards. Initially, my thought process is too literal and I'm overly focused on the subject matter. But after a few days of staring and deleting and recombining, I can see a certain rhythm. I lay out three photos of Dal Lake that I made from the roof deck of my houseboat in Srinagar, each one taken at a different time on different days. The east-facing view is too similar so I plan to choose only one of them. And then it hits me — like one of those visual puzzles that suddenly reveals itself as you stare — that the three photos line up. After I move the purple-hued photo into the middle, the line of the mountains tracks across the prints. The distinct color tone of each photo suggests a different time of day. I've created a panoramic image of the lake — accidental, beautiful and strange. I think back to arriving on the houseboat and all of the peculiar and revelatory moments that followed. A mystic thread emerges and subtly works its way through the photographs in front of me.

Book published by
Patricio Binaghi for Paripé Books
paripebooks.com

Photographs by
Brian W. Ferry
brianwferry.com

Art Direction by
Cristian Ordóñez
cristianordonez.com

First Edition of 1000 copies
Printed in 2017 in Toronto, Canada
All photographs and text copyright 2017 Brian W. Ferry

THANK YOU to Gulzar Hussein, Leonor Mamanna, Jennifer Miller, Dan Bailey, Condé Nast Traveler, Jonás Romo, Valeda Stull, Lynsey Waite, Anil Kumar at Bleeker Photo, Pablo Budeisky, Cristian Ordóñez for his creativity and patience, and Patricio Binaghi for all of his support.

All rights reserved. No part of this publication may be reprinted, reproduced or transmitted in any form without the written permission of the authors and the publisher.

ISBN 13: 978-84-947238-0-3